D1707819

EMERSON
ON MAN &
GOD

PETER PAUPER PRESS
MOUNT VERNON · NEW YORK

RALPH WALDO EMERSON

ON MAN AND GOD

.   .   .

THOUGHTS COLLECTED
FROM THE ESSAYS
AND JOURNALS

ON SELF-RELIANCE

❦ Whoso would be a man, must be a noncon-formist. He who would gather mortal palms must not be hindered by the name of good-ness, but must explore if it be goodness. Nothing is at last sacred but the integrity of your own mind. Absolve you to yourself, and you shall have the suffrage of the world.

℃ Difficulties exist to be surmounted. The great heart will no more complain of the obstructions that make success hard, than of the iron walls of the gun which hinder the shot from scattering. It was walled round with iron tube with that purpose, to give it irresistible force in one direction. A strenuous soul hates cheap successes.

℃ A man never gets acquainted with himself, but is always a surprise. We get news daily of the world within, as well as of the world outside, and not less of the central than of the surface facts. A new thought is awaiting him every morning.

℃ Books are the best of things, well used; abused, among the worst. What is the right use? What is the one end which all means go to effect? They are for nothing but to inspire. I had better never see a book than to be warped by its attraction clean out of my own orbit, and made a satellite instead of a system.

℃ To believe your own thought, to believe that what is true for you in your private heart is true for all men — that is genius. Speak your latent conviction, and it shall be the universal sense; for the inmost in due time becomes the outmost, and our first thought is rendered back to us by the trumpets of the Last Judgment.

❤ God offers to every mind its choice between truth and repose. Take which you please — you can never have both. Between these, as a pendulum, man oscillates. He in whom the love of repose predominates will accept the first creed, the first philosophy, the first political party he meets — most likely his father's. He gets rest, commodity and reputation; but he shuts the door of truth. He in whom the love of truth predominates will keep himself aloof from all moorings, and afloat. He will abstain from dogmatism, and recognize all the opposite negations between which, as walls, his being is swung. He submits to the inconvenience of suspense and imperfect opinion.

❤ The great majority of men are not original, for they are not primary, have not assumed their own vows, but are secondaries — grow up and grow old in seeming and following; and when they die they occupy themselves to the last with what others will think, and whether Mr. A and Mr. B will go to their funeral.

❤ A man is furnished with this superb case of instruments, the senses, and perceptive and executive faculties, and they betray him every day. He transfers his allegiance from Instinct and God to this adroit little committee.

❡ Yesterday I went to the Athenaeum and looked through journals and books — for wit, for excitement, to wake in me the muse. In vain, and in vain. And am I yet to learn that the God dwells within? That books are but crutches, the resorts of the feeble and lame, which, if used by the strong, weaken the muscular power, and become necessary aids.

❡ No law can be sacred to me but that of my nature. Good and bad are but names very readily transferable to that or this; the only right is what is after my constitution; the only wrong what is against it. A man is to carry himself in the presence of all opposition as if everything were titular and ephemeral but he. I am ashamed to think how easily we capitulate to badges and names, to large societies and dead institutions.

❡ The Saharas must be crossed as well as the Nile. It is easy to live for others; everybody does. I call on you to live for yourselves, so shall you find in this penury and absence of thought a purer splendor than ever clothed the exhibitions of wit.

❡ There is no history. There is only biography. The attempt to perpetrate, to fix a thought or principle, fails continually. You can only live for yourself; your action is good only whilst it is alive — whilst it is in you. The awkward imitation of it by your child or your disciple is not a repetition of it, is not the same thing, but another thing. The new individual must work out the whole problem of science, letters and theology for himself; can owe his fathers nothing. There is no history; only biography.

❧ Patience and patience, we shall win at the last. We must be very suspicious of the deceptions of the element of time. It takes a good deal of time to eat or to sleep, or to earn a hundred dollars, and a very little time to entertain a hope and an insight which becomes the light of our life. We dress our garden, eat our dinners, discuss the household with our wives, and these things make no impression, are forgotten next week; but, in the solitude to which every man is always returning, he has a sanity and revelations which in his passage into new worlds he will carry with him. Never mind the ridicule, never mind the defeat; up again, old heart! — it seems to say, there is victory yet for all justice; and the true romance which the world exists to realize will be the transformation of genius into practical power.

❧ The spirit of the American freeman is already suspected to be timid, imitative, tame. Public and private avarice make the air we breathe thick and fat. The scholar is decent, indolent, complaisant. See already the tragic consequences. The mind of this country, taught to aim at low objects, eats upon itself. There is no work for any but the decorous and the complaisant. Young men of the fairest promise, who begin life upon our shores, inflated by the mountain winds, shined upon by all the stars of God, find the earth below not in unison with these, but are hindered from action by the disgust which the principles on which business is managed inspire, and turn drudges, or die of disgust, some of them suicides. What is the remedy? They did not yet see, and thousands of young men as hopeful now crowding to the barriers for the career do not yet see, that if the single man plant himself indomitably on his instincts, and there abide, the huge world will come round to him.

❲ A foolish consistency is the hobgoblin of little minds, adored by little statesmen and philosophers and divines. With consistency a great soul has simply nothing to do. He may as well concern himself with his shadow on the wall. Speak what you think now in hard words and tomorrow speak what tomorrow thinks in hard words again, though it contradict everything you said today.

TRANSCENDENTALISM

❦ I conceive a man as always spoken to from behind, and unable to turn his head and see the speaker. In all the millions who have heard the voice, none ever saw the face. As children in their play run behind each other, and seize one by the ears and make him walk before them, so is the spirit of our unseen pilot.

❡ That well-known voice speaks in all languages, governs all men, and none ever caught a glimpse of its form. If the man will exactly obey it, it will adopt him, so that he shall not any longer separate it from himself in his thought; he shall seem to be it, he shall be it. If he listen with insatiable ears, richer and greater wisdom is taught him; the sound swells to a ravishing music, he is borne away as with a flood, he becomes careless of his food and of his house, he is the fool of ideas, and leads a heavenly life. But if his eye is set on the things to be done, and not on the truth that is still taught, and for the sake of which the things are to be done, then the voice grows faint, and at last is but a humming in his ears. His health and greatness consist in his being the channel through which heaven flows to earth.

❡ I write laboriously after a law, which I see, and then lose, and then see again. And, I doubt not, though I see around me many men of superior talent, that my reader will do me the justice to feel that I am not contriving something to surprise or to tickle him, but am seriously striving to say that which is.

❡ This power of imagination, the making of some familiar object, as fire or rain, or a bucket, or shovel do new duty as an exponent

of some truth or general law, bewitches and delights men. It is a taking of dead sticks, and clothing about with immortality; it is music out of creaking and scouring. All opaque things are transparent, and the light of heaven struggles through.

℘ I cannot see without awe that no man thinks alone and no man acts alone, but the divine assessors who came up with him into life — now under one disguise, now under another, like a police in citizens' clothes — walk with him, step for step, through all the kingdom of time.

℘ Where do we find ourselves? In a series of which we do not know the extremes, and believe that it has none. We wake and find ourselves on a stair; there are stairs below us, which we seem to have ascended; there are stairs above us, many a one, which go upward and out of sight.

℘ The best part of every mind is not that which he knows, but that which hovers in gleams, suggestions, tantalizing, unpossessed, before him. His firm recorded knowledge soon loses all interest for him. But this dancing chorus of thoughts and hopes is the quarry of his future, is his possibility, and teaches him that his man's life is of a ridiculous brevity and meanness.

❡ Am I not, one of these days, to write consecutively of the beatitude of intellect? It is too great for feeble souls, and they are overexcited. The wine-glass shakes, and the wine is spilled. What then? The joy which will not let me sit in my chair, which brings me bolt upright to my feet, and sends me striding around my room, like a tiger in his cage, and I cannot have composure and concentration enough even to set down in English words the thought which thrills me — is not that joy a certificate of the elevation?

❡ How wild and mysterious our position as individuals to the Universe; here is always a certain amount of truth lodged as intrinsic foundation in the depths of the soul, a certain perception of absolute being, as justice, love, and the like, natures which must be the God of God, and this is our capital stock, this is our centripetal force.

❡ As a plant upon the earth, so a man rests upon the bosom of God; he is nourished by unfailing fountains, and draws at his need inexhaustible power. Who can set bounds to the possibilities of man? Once inhale the upper air, being admitted to behold the absolute natures of justice and truth, and we learn that man has access to the entire mind of the Creator, is himself the creator in the finite.

❦ On its own level, or in view of nature, temperament is final. I see not, if one be once caught in this trap of so-called sciences, any escape for the man from the links of the chain of physical necessity. Given such an embryo, such a history must follow. On this platform one lives in a sty of sensualism, and would soon come to suicide. But it is impossible that the creative power should exclude itself. Into every intelligence there is a door which is never closed, through which the creator passes. The intellect, seeker of absolute truth, or the heart, lover of absolute good, intervenes for our succor, and at one whisper of these high powers we awake from ineffectual struggles with this nightmare. We hurl it into its own hell, and cannot again contract ourselves to so base a state.

❦ Men go through the world each musing on a great fable, dramatically pictured and rehearsed before him. If you speak to the man, he turns his eyes from his own scene, and slower or faster endeavors to comprehend what you say. When you have done speaking, he returns to his private music.

THERE IS A THREAD...

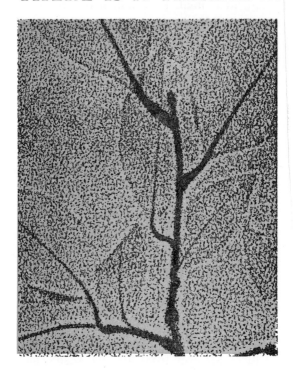

❡ We are natural believers. Truth, or the con-nection between cause and effect, alone in-terests us. We are persuaded that a thread runs through all things: all worlds are strung on it, as beads; and men, and events, and life, come to us only because of that thread: they pass and repass only that we may know the direction and continuity of that line.

❲ I ask not for the great, the remote, the romantic; what is doing in Italy or Arabia; what is Greek art, or Provençal minstrelsy; I embrace the common, I explore and sit at the feet of the familiar, the low. Give me insight into today, and you may have the antique and future worlds. What would we really know the meaning of? The meal in the firkin; the milk in the pan; the ballad in the street; the news of the boat; the glance of the eye; the form and the gait of the body — show me the ultimate reason of these matters; show me the sublime presence of the highest spiritual cause lurking, as always it does lurk, in these suburbs and extremities of nature; let me see every trifle bristling with the polarity that ranges it instantly on an eternal law; and the shop, the plough, and the ledger referred to the like cause by which light undulates and poets sing — and the world lies no longer a dull miscellany and lumber-room, but has form and order; there is no trifle, there is no puzzle, but one design unites and animates the farthest pinnacle and the lowest trench.

❲ I dreamed that I floated at will in the great Ether, and I saw this world floating also not far off, but diminished to the size of an apple. Then an angel took it in his hand and brought it to me and said, "This must thou eat." And I ate the world.

❦ The instincts of the ant are very unimportant considered as the ant's; but the moment a ray of relation is seen to extend from it to man, and the little drudge is seen to be a monitor, a little body with a mighty heart, then all its habits, even that said to be recently observed, that it never sleeps, become sublime.

❦ The truth takes flesh in forms that can express it; and thus in history an idea always overhangs, like the moon, and rules the tide which rises simultaneously in all the souls of a generation.

❦ A life in harmony with Nature, the love of truth and of virtue, will purge the eyes to understand her text. By degrees we may come to know the primitive sense of the permanent objects of nature, so that the world shall be to us an open book, and every form significant of its hidden life and final cause.

❦ The moral law lies at the center of nature and radiates to the circumference. It is the pith and marrow of every substance, every relation, and every process. All things with which we deal, preach to us. What is a farm but a mute gospel? The chaff and the wheat, weeds and plants, blight, rain, insects, sun — it is a sacred emblem from the first furrow of spring to the last stack which the snow of winter overtakes in the fields.

❲ The great man knew not that he was great. It took a century or two for that fact to appear. What he did, he did because he must; it was the most natural thing in the world, and grew out of the circumstances of the moment. But now, every thing he did, even to the lifting of his finger or the eating of bread, looks large, all-related, and is called an institution.

❲ The world globes itself in a drop of dew. The microscope cannot find the animalcule which is less perfect for being little. Eyes, ears, taste, smell, motion, resistance, appetite, and organs of reproduction that take hold on eternity — all find room to consist in the small creature. So do we put our life into every act.

❲ I have seen in the sky a chain of summer lightning which at once showed to me that the Greeks drew from nature when they painted the thunderbolt in the hand of Jove. I have seen a snow-drift along the sides of the stone wall which obviously gave the idea of the common architectural scroll to abut a tower.

❲ The difference of circumstance is merely costume. I am tasting the self-same life — its sweetness, its greatness, its pain, which I so admire in other men. Do not foolishly ask of the inscrutable, obliterated past, what it cannot tell — the details of that nature, of that day, called Byron, or Burke — but ask it of the enveloping Now; the more quaintly you inspect its evanescent beauties, its wonderful details, its spiritual causes, its astounding whole — so much the more you master the biography of this hero, and that, and every hero. Be lord of a day, through wisdom and justice, and you can put up your history books.

❦ The feat of the imagination is in showing the convertibility of every thing into every other thing. Facts which had never before left their stark common sense suddenly figure as Eleusinian mysteries. My boots and chair and candlestick are fairies in disguise, meteors and constellations. All the facts in nature are nouns of the intellect, and make the grammar of the eternal language.

❦ The world is emblematic. Parts of speech are metaphors, because the whole of nature is a metaphor of the human mind. The laws of moral nature answer to those of matter as face to face in a glass.

❦ Each creature is only a modification of the other; the likeness in them is more than the difference, and their radical law is one and the same. A rule of one art, or a law of one organization, holds true throughout nature.

NATURE AS BEAUTY

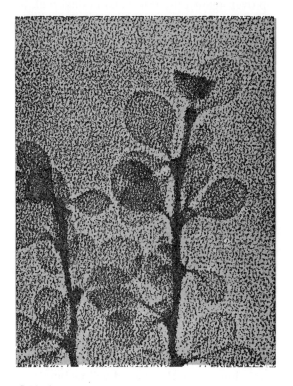

❨ If the stars should appear one night in a thousand years, how would men believe and adore; and preserve for many generations the remembrance of the city of God which had been shown! But every night come out these envoys of beauty, and light the universe with their admonishing smile.

❧ I see the spectacle of morning from the hill-top over against my house, from daybreak to sunrise, with emotions which an angel might share. The long slender bars of cloud float like fishes in the sea of crimson light. From the earth, as a shore, I look out into that silent sea. I seem to partake its rapid transformations; the active enchantment reaches my dust, and I dilate and conspire with the morning wind. How does nature deify us with a few and cheap elements! Give me health and a day, and I will make the pomp of emperors ridiculous.

❧ The world wears well. These autumn afternoons and well-marbled landscapes of green and gold and russet, and steel-blue river, and smoke-blue New Hampshire mountains, are and remain as bright and perfect pencilling as ever.

❧ The hurts of the husbandmen are many. As soon as the heat bursts his vine-seed and the cotyledons open, the striped yellow bugs and the stupid squash-bug, smelling like a decomposing pear, sting the little plants to death and destroy the hope of melons. And as soon as the grass is well cut and spread on the ground, the thunderclouds, which are the bugs of the haymakers, come growling down the heaven and make tea of his hay.

℃ The man who has seen the rising moon break out of the clouds at midnight, has been present like an archangel at the creation of light and of the world.

℃ It is curious that we so peremptorily require beauty, and if it do not exist in anyone, we feel at liberty to insult over that subject, without end. Thus the poor Donkey is not handsome, and so is the gibe of all mankind in all ages, notwithstanding his eminent usefulness; whilst those handsome cats, the lion, leopard, tiger are allowed to tear and devour because handsome mischiefs, and are the badges of kings.

℃ I too have a new plaything, the best I ever had — a woodlot. Last fall I bought a piece of more than forty acres, on the border of a little lake half a mile wide and more, called Walden Pond — a place to which my feet have for years been accustomed to bring me once or twice a week at all seasons.

℃ Not the sun or the summer alone, but every hour and season yields its tribute of delight; for every hour and change corresponds to and authorizes a different state of the mind, from breathless noon to grimmest midnight. Nature is a setting that fits equally well a comic or a mourning piece.

❡ Nature . . . does not like our benevolence or our learning much better than she likes our frauds and wars. When we come out of the caucus, or the bank, or the Abolition-convention, or the Temperance-meeting, or the Transcendental club into the fields and woods, she says to us, "So hot? my little Sir."

❡ Few men know how to take a walk. The qualifications of a professor are endurance, plain clothes, old shoes, an eye for Nature, good humor, vast curiosity, good speech, good silence and nothing too much. If a man tells me that he has an intense love of Nature, I know, of course, that he has none. Good observers have the manners of trees and animals, their patient good sense, and if they add words, 'tis only when words are better than silence.

❡ A work of art is an abstract or epitome of the world. It is the result or expression of nature, in miniature. For although the works of nature are innumerable and all different, the result or the expression of them all is similar and single. Nature is a sea of forms radically alike and even unique. A leaf, a sunbeam, a landscape, the ocean, make an analogous impression on the mind. What is common to them all, that perfectness and harmony, is beauty.

LOVE & FRIENDSHIP

℄ We are armed all over with subtle antagonisms, which, as soon as we meet, begin to play, and translate all poetry into stale prose. Almost all people descend to meet. All association must be a compromise, and, what is worst, the very flower and aroma of the flower of each of the beautiful natures disappears as they approach each other.

❦ I do then with my friends as I do with my books. I would have them where I can find them, but I seldom use them. We must have society on our own terms, and admit or exclude it on the slightest cause. I cannot afford to speak much with my friend. If he is great he makes me so great that I cannot descend to converse.

❦ If the tone of the companion is higher than ours, we delight in rising to it. 'Tis a historic observation that a writer must find an audience up to his thought, or he will no longer care to impart it, but will sink to their level or be silent.

❦ Your goodness must have some edge to it — else it is none. The doctrine of hatred must be preached, as the counteraction of the doctrine of love, when that pules and whines. I shun father and mother and wife and brother when my genius calls me. I would write on the lintels of the door-post, *Whim*. I hope it is somewhat better than whim at last, but we cannot spend the day in explanation.

❦ Solitude is impracticable, and society fatal. We must keep our head in the one and our hands in the other. The conditions are met, if we keep our independence, yet do not lose our sympathy. These wonderful horses need to be driven by fine hands.

℄ Nature wishes that woman should attract man, yet she often cunningly moulds into her face a little sarcasm, which seems to say, "Yes, I am willing to attract, but to attract a little better kind of man than any I yet behold."

℄ Love is necessary to the righting the estate of woman in this world. Otherwise nature itself seems to be in conspiracy against her dignity and welfare; for the cultivated, high-thoughted, beauty-loving, saintly woman finds herself unconsciously desired for her sex, and even enhancing the appetite of her savage pursuers by these fine ornaments she has piously laid on herself. She finds with indignation that she is herself a snare, and was made such. I do not wonder at her occasional protest, violent protest against nature, in fleeing to nunneries, and taking black veils. Love rights all this deep wrong.

℄ I wish my house to be a college, open as the air to all to whom I spiritually belong, and who belong to me. But it is not open to others, or for other purposes. I do not wish that it should be a confectioner's shop wherein eaters and drinkers may get strawberries and champagne. I do not wish that it should be a playground or house of entertainment for boys. They do well to play; I like that they should, but not with me, or in these precincts.

℃ I finish this morning transcribing my old essay on Love, but I see well its inadequateness. I, cold because I am hot — cold at the surface only as a sort of guard and compensation for the fluid tenderness of the core — have much more experience than I have written there, more than I will, more than I can write.

℃ It is not the office of a man to receive gifts. How dare you give them? We wish to be self-sustained. We do not quite forgive a giver. The hand that feeds us is in some danger of being bitten. We can receive anything from love, for that is a way of receiving it from ourselves; but not from anyone who assumes to bestow. We sometimes hate the meat which we eat, because there seems something of degrading dependence in living by it.

℃ Every man alone is sincere. At the entrance of a second person, hypocrisy begins. We parry and fend the approach of our fellow-man by compliments, by gossip, by amusements, by affairs.

℃ I spoke of friendship, but my friends and I are fishes in our habit. As for taking Thoreau's arm, I should as soon take the arm of an elm tree.

AMERICA & POLITICS

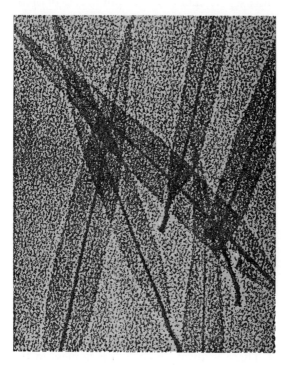

❈ The spirit of our American radicalism is destructive and aimless: it is not loving; it has no ulterior and divine ends, but is destructive only out of hatred and selfishness. On the other side, the conservative party, composed of the most moderate, able and cultivated part of the population, is timid, and merely defensive of property.

❡ The timidity of our public opinion is our disease, or, shall I say, the publicness of opinion, the absence of private opinion. Good nature is plentiful, but we want justice, with heart of steel, to fight down the proud. The private mind has the access to the totality of goodness and truth that it may be a balance to a corrupt society; and to stand for the private verdict against popular clamor is the office of the noble. If a humane measure is propounded in behalf of the slave, or of the Irishman, or the Catholic, or for the succor of the poor; that sentiment, that project, will have the homage of the hero.

❡ The office of America is to liberate, to abolish kingcraft, priestcraft, caste, monopoly, to pull down the gallows, to burn up the bloody statute-book, to take in the immigrant, to open the doors of the sea and the fields of the earth.

❡ There is always a certain meanness in the argument of conservatism, joined with a certain superiority in its fact. It affirms because it holds. Its fingers clutch the fact, and it will not open its eyes to see a better fact. The castle which conservatism is set to defend is the actual state of things, good and bad. The project of innovation is the best possible state of things.

❦ Fear for ages has boded and mowed and gibbered over government and property. That obscene bird is not there for nothing. He indicates great wrongs which must be revised.

❦ America is formless, has no terrible and no beautiful condensation. Genius, always anthropomorphist, runs every idea into a fable, constructs, finishes, as the plastic Italian cannot build a post or a pump-handle but it terminates in a human head.

❦ Thoreau was in his own person a practical answer, almost a refutation, to the theories of the socialists. He required no Phalanx, no Government, no society, almost no memory. He lived extempore from hour to hour, like the birds and the angels; brought every day a new proposition, as revolutionary as that of yesterday, but different: the only man of leisure in his town; and his independence made all others look like slaves.

❦ Hell is better than Heaven, if the man in Hell knows his place, and the man in Heaven does not. It is in vain you pretend that you are not responsible for the evil law because you are not a magistrate, or a party to a civil process, or do not vote. You eat the law in a crust of bread, you wear it in your hat and shoes. The Man — it is his attitude: the attitude makes the man.

❧ If there is any period one would desire to be born in, is it not the age of Revolution; when the old and the new stand side by side and admit of being compared; when the energies of all men are searched by fear and by hope; when the historic glories of the old can be compensated by the rich possibilities of the new era?

❧ Eager, solicitous, hungry, rabid, busy-bodied America attempting many things, vain, ambitious to feel thy own existence, and convince others of thy talent, by attempting and hastily accomplishing much; yes, catch thy breath and correct thyself, and failing here, prosper out there; speed and fever are never greatness; but reliance and serenity and waiting.

❧ Masses! the calamity is the masses. I do not wish any mass at all, but honest men only, lovely, sweet, accomplished women only, and no shovel-handed, narrow-brained, gin-drinking million stockingers or lazzaroni at all. If government knew how, I should like to see it check, not multiply the population. When it reaches its true law of action, every man that is born will be hailed as essential. Away with this hurrah of masses, and let us have the considerate vote of single men spoken on their honor and their conscience.

❆ Is it not better to live in Revolution than live in dead times? Are we not little and lo out of good nature now, when, if our companions were noble, or the crisis fit for heroes, we should be great also?

❆ The history of persecution is a history of endeavors to cheat nature, to make water run up hill, to twist a rope of sand. It makes no difference whether the actors be many or one, a tyrant or a mob. A mob is a society of bodies voluntarily bereaving themselves of reason and traversing its work. The mob is man voluntarily descending to the nature of the beast. Its fit hour of activity is night.

❆ Why are the masses, from the dawn of history down, food for knives and powder? The idea dignifies a few leaders, who have sentiment, opinion, love, self-devotion; and they make war and death sacred — but what for the wretches whom they hire and kill? The cheapness of man is every day's tragedy. It is as real a loss that others should be low as that we should be low; for we must have society.

❆ The less government we have the better — the fewer laws, and the less confided power. The antidote to this abuse of formal government is the influence of private character, the growth of the Individual.

❦ The State is a poor, good beast who means the best: it means friendly. A poor cow who does well by you — do not grudge it its hay. It cannot eat bread, as you can; let it have without grudge a little grass for its four stomachs. It will not stint to yield you milk from its teat. You, who are a man walking cleanly on two feet, will not pick a quarrel with a poor cow. Take this handful of clover and welcome. But if you go to hook me when I walk in the fields, then, poor cow, I will cut your throat.

❦ All our political disasters grow as logically out of our attempts in the past to do without justice, as the sinking of some part of your house comes to defect in the foundation. One thing is plain; a certain personal virtue is essential to freedom; and it begins to be doubtful whether our corruption in this country has not gone a little over the mark of safety, so that when canvassed we shall be found to be made up of a majority of reckless self-seekers. The divine knowledge has ebbed out of us and we do not know enough to be free.

SOBERING REALITIES

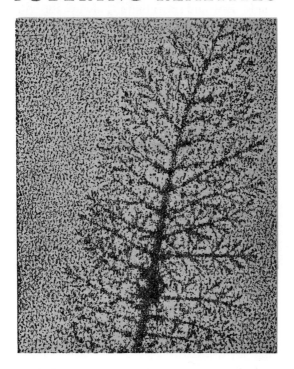

❦ A man cannot utter two or three sentences without disclosing to intelligent ears precisely where he stands in life and thought, namely, whether in the kingdom of the senses and the understanding, or in that of ideas and imagination, in the realm of intuitions and duty. People seem not to see that their opinion of the world is also a confession of character.

❲ There is a crack in everything God has made. It would seem there is always this vindictive circumstance stealing in at unawares even into the wild poesy in which the human fancy attempted to make bold holiday and to shake itself free of the old laws — this backstroke, this kick of the gun, certifying that the law is fatal; that in nature nothing can be given, all things are sold.

❲ The world is full of renunciations and apprenticeships, and this is thine; thou must pass for a fool and a churl for a long season. This is the screen and sheath in which Pan has protected his well-beloved flower, and thou shalt be known only to thine own, and they shall console thee with tenderest love.

❲ There are people who have an appetite for grief, pleasure is not strong enough and they crave pain, mithridatic stomachs which must be fed on poisoned bread, natures so doomed that no prosperity can soothe their ragged and disheveled desolation. They mis-hear and mis-behold, they suspect and dread. They handle every nettle and ivy in the hedge, and tread on every snake in the meadow.

❲ Among the lovers of the new I observe that there is a jealousy of the newest, and that the seceder from the seceder is as damnable as the pope himself.

❦ The scholar blunders along on his own path for a time, assured by the surprise and joy of those to whom he first communicates his results; then new solitudes, new marches; but after a time, on looking up he finds the sympathy gone or changed, he fancies himself accused by all the bystanders; the faces of his friends are shaded by grief; and yet no tongue ever speaks of the cause.

❦ Meek young men grow up in libraries, believing it their duty to accept the views which Cicero, which Locke, which Bacon, have given; forgetful that Cicero, Locke, and Bacon were only young men in libraries when they wrote these books. Hence, instead of Man Thinking, we have the bookworm. Hence the book-learned class, who value books, as such; not as related to nature and the human constitution, but as making a sort of Third Estate with the world and the soul.

❦ One would think from the talk of men that riches and poverty were a great matter; and our civilization mainly respects it. But the Indians say that they do not think the white man, with his brow of care, always toiling, afraid of heat and cold, and keeping within doors, has any advantage of them. The permanent interest of every man is never to be in a false position, but to have the weight of nature to back him in all that he does. Riches and poverty are a thick or thin costume.

℃ Neither will poverty suit every complexion. Socrates and Franklin may well go hungry and in plain clothes, if they like; but there are people who cannot afford this, but whose poverty of nature needs wealth of food and clothes to make them decent.

℃ A man must consider what a blind-man's-buff is this game of conformity. If I know your sect I anticipate your argument. I hear a preacher announce for his text and topic the expediency of one of the institutions of his church. Do I not know beforehand that not possibly can he say a new and spontaneous word? Do I not know that with all this ostentation of examining the grounds of the institution he will do no such thing? Do I not know that he is pledged to himself not to look but at one side, the permitted side, not as a man, but as a parish minister? He is a retained attorney, and these airs of the bench are the emptiest affectation.

℃ The existence of evil and malignant men does not depend on themselves or on men; it indicates the virulence that still remains uncured in the universe, uncured and corrupting, and hurling out these pestilent rats and tigers, and men rat-like and wolf-like.

❡ We are very careful of young pear trees and defend them from their enemies, from fire, blight, suckers, grass, slugs, pear-worm, but we let our young men, in whose youth and flower all inferior kinds have their flowering and completion, grow up in heaps and by chance, take the rough and tumble, as we say (which is the skepticism of Education), exposed to their borers, caterpillars, cankerworms, bugs, moping, sloth, seduction, wine, fear, hatred.

❡ For nonconformity the world whips you with its displeasure. And therefore a man must know how to estimate a sour face. The by-standers look askance on him in the public street or in the friend's parlor. If this aversion had its origin in contempt and resistance like his own he might well go home with a sad countenance; but the sour faces of the multitude, like their sweet faces, have no deep cause, but are put on and off as the wind blows and a newspaper directs.

❡ As long as our civilization is essentially one of property, of fences, of exclusiveness, it will be mocked by delusions. Our riches will leave us sick; there will be bitterness in our laughter, and our wine will burn our mouth. Only that good profits which we can taste with all doors open, and which serves all men.

THE CREATIVE ACT

❡ Though the origin of most of our words is forgotten, each word was at first a stroke of genius, and obtained currency because for the moment it symbolized the world to the first speaker and to the hearer. The etymologist finds the deadest word to have been once a brilliant picture. Language is fossil poetry.

❦ The toper finds, without asking, the road to the tavern, but the poet does not know the pitcher that holds his nectar. Every youth should know the way to prophecy as surely as the miller understands how to let on the water or the engineer the steam. A rush of thoughts is the only conceivable prosperity that can come to us. Fine clothes, equipages, villa, park, social consideration, cannot cover up real poverty and insignificance, from my own eyes or from others like mine.

❦ It will not need, when the mind is prepared for study, to search for objects. The invariable mark of wisdom is to see the miraculous in the common. What is a day? What is a year? What is summer? What is woman? What is a child? What is sleep?

❦ The art of the writer is to speak his fact and have done. Let the reader find that he cannot afford to omit any line of your writing, because you have omitted every word that he can spare.

❦ Happy is he who looks only into his work to know if it will succeed, never into the times or the public opinion; and who writes from the love of imparting certain thoughts and not from the necessity of sale — who writes always to *the unknown friend.*

❧ The maker of a sentence, like the other artist, launches out into the infinite and builds a road into Chaos and old Night, and is followed by those who hear him with something of a wild, creative delight.

❧ Wit makes its own welcome, and levels all distinctions. No dignity, no learning, no force of character, can make any stand against good wit. It is like ice, on which no beauty of form, no majesty of carriage can plead any immunity — they must walk gingerly, according to the laws of ice, or down they must go, dignity and all.

❧ The moment our discourse rises above the ground line of familiar facts and is inflamed with passion or exalted by thought, it clothes itself in images. . . . Hence, good writing and brilliant discourse are perpetual allegories. This imagery is spontaneous. It is the blending of experience with the present action of the mind. It is proper creation. It is the working of the Original Cause through the instruments he has already made.

❧ Thought makes everything fit for use. The vocabulary of an omniscient man would embrace words and images excluded from polite conversation. What would be base, or even obscene, to the obscene, becomes illustrious, spoken in a new connection of thought.

❦ Proverbs, like the sacred books of each nation, are the sanctuary of the intuitions. That which the droning world, chained to appearances, will not allow the realist to say in his own words, it will suffer him to say in proverbs without contradiction.

❦ For the instinct is sure, that prompts him to tell his brother what he thinks. He then learns that in going down into the secrets of his own mind he has descended into the secrets of all minds. He learns that he who has mastered any law in his private thoughts, is master to that extent of all men whose language he speaks, and of all into whose language his own can be translated. The poet, in utter solitude remembering his spontaneous thoughts and recording them, is found to have recorded that which men in crowded cities find true for them also.

❦ The artists must be sacrificed to their art. Like bees, they must put their lives into the sting they give. What is a man good for without enthusiasm? and what is enthusiasm but this daring of ruin for its object? There are thoughts beyond the reaches of our souls; we are not the less drawn to them. The moth flies into the flame of the lamp; and Swedenborg must solve the problems that haunt him, though he be crazed or killed.

℃ Our admiration of the antique is not admiration of the old, but of the natural. The Greeks are not reflective, but perfect in their senses and in their health, with the finest physical organization in the world. Adults acted with the simplicity and grace of children. They made vases, tragedies and statues, such as healthy senses should — that is, in good taste. . . . They combine the energy of manhood with the engaging unconsciousness of childhood.

℃ A man's power to connect his thought with its proper symbol, and so to utter it, depends on the simplicity of his character, that is, upon his love of truth and his desire to communicate it without loss. The corruption of man is followed by the corruption of language.

℃ In every work of genius we recognize our own rejected thoughts; they come back to us with a certain alienated majesty. Great works of art have no more affecting lesson for us than this. They teach us to abide by our spontaneous impression with good-humored inflexibility then most when the whole cry of voices is on the other side. Else tomorrow a stranger will say with masterly good sense precisely what we have thought and felt all the time, and we shall be forced to take with shame our own opinion from another.

❡ It is singular that wherever we find a man higher by a whole head than any of his contemporaries, it is sure to come into doubt what are his real words. Thus Homer, Plato, Raffaelle, Shakespeare. For these men magnetize their contemporaries, so that their companions can do for them what they can never do for themselves; and the great man does thus live in several bodies, and write, or paint or act, by many hands; and after some time it is not easy to say what is the authentic work of the master and what is only of his school.

❡ There is less intention in history than we ascribe to it. We impute keep-laid far-sighted plans to Cæsar and Napoleon; but the best of their power was in nature, not in them. . . . Their success lay in their parallelism to the course of thought, which found in them an unobstructed channel; and the wonders of which they were the visible conductors seemed to the eye their deed.

❡ It is easy to sugar to be sweet and to nitre to be salt. We take a great deal of pains to waylay and entrap that which of itself will fall into our hands. I count him a great man who inhabits a higher sphere of thought, into which other men rise with labor and difficulty; he has but to open his eyes to see things in a true light and in large relations.

ℂ Nature makes fifty poor melons for one that is good, and shakes down a tree full of gnarled, wormy, unripe crabs, before you can find a dozen dessert apples; and she scatters nations of naked Indians and nations of clothed Christians, with two or three good heads among them. Nature works very hard, and only hits the white once in a million throws. In mankind she is contented if she yields one master in a century. The more difficulty there is in creating good men, the more they are used when they come.

ℂ The imbecility of men is always inviting the impudence of power. It is the delight of vulgar talent to dazzle and to blind the beholder. But true genius seeks to defend us from itself.

ℂ I believe man has been wronged; he has wronged himself. He has almost lost the light that can lead him back to his prerogatives. Men are become of no account. Men in history, men in the world of today, are bugs, are spawn, and are called "the mass" and "the herd." In a century, in a millennium, one or two men; that is to say, one or two approximations to the right state of every man.

ℂ I cannot tell what I would know; but I have observed there are persons who, in their character and actions, answer questions which I have not skill to put.

❦ Great men serve us as insurrections do in bad governments. The world would run into endless routine, and forms incrust forms, till the life was gone. But the perpetual supply of new genius shocks us with thrills of life, and recalls us to principles.

❦ The poor and the low find some amends to their immense moral capacity, for their acquiescence in a political and social inferiority. They are content to be brushed like flies from the path of a great person, so that justice shall be done by him to that common nature which it is the dearest desire of all to see enlarged and glorified. They sun themselves in the great man's light, and feel it to be their own element. They cast the dignity of man from their downtrod selves upon the shoulders of a hero, and will perish to add one drop of blood to make that great heart beat, those giant sinews combat and conquer. He lives for us, and we live in him.

❦ It is natural to believe in great men. If the companions of our childhood should turn out to be heroes, and their condition regal it would not surprise us.

ON R.W.E. HIMSELF

❧ When I was thirteen years old, my Uncle Samuel Ripley one day asked me, "How is it, Ralph, that all the boys dislike you and quarrel with you, whilst the grown people are fond of you?" Now am I thirty-six and the fact is reversed — the old people suspect and dislike me, and the young love me.

❡ *Dreams.* I owe real knowledge and even alarming hints to dreams, and wonder to see people extracting emptiness from mahogany tables, when there is vatication in their dreams. For the soul in dreams has a subtle synthetic power which it will not exert under the sharp eyes of days.

❡ I am here at work now for a fortnight to spin some single cord out of my thousand and one strands of every color and texture that lie raveled around me in old snarls. We need to be possessed with a mountainous conviction of the value of our advice to our contemporaries, if we will take such pains to find what that is.

❡ I think myself more a man than some men I know, inasmuch as I see myself to be open to the enjoyment of talents and deeds of other men, as they are not. When a talent comes by, which I cannot appreciate and other men can, I instantly am inferior. With all my ears I cannot detect unity or plan in a strain of Beethoven. Here is a man who draws from it a frank delight. So much is he more a man than I.

❡ We do not determine what we will think. We only open our senses, clear away as we call all obstruction from the fact, and suffer the intellect to see. We have little control over our thoughts. We are the prisoners of ideas.

❧ I please myself with getting my nail-box set in the snuggest corner of the barn-chamber and well filled with nails, and gimlet, pincers, screwdriver and chisel. Herein I find an old joy of youth, of childhood, which perhaps all domestic children share — the catlike love of garrets, barns and corn-chambers, and of the conveniences of long housekeeping.

❧ Like the New England soil, my talent is good only whilst I work it. If I cease to task myself, I have no thoughts. This is a poor sterile Yankeeism. What I admire and love is the generous and spontaneous soil which flowers and fruits at all seasons.

❧ I have usually read that a man suffered more from one hard word than he enjoyed from ten good ones. My own experience does not confirm the saying. The censure (I either know or fancy) does not hit me; and the praise is very good.

❧ You sometimes charge me with I know not what sky-blue, sky-void idealism. As far as it is a partiality, I fear I may be more deeply infected than you think me. I have very joyful dreams which I cannot bring to paper, much less to any approach to practice, and I blame myself not at all for my reveries, but that they have not yet got possession of my house and barn.

❡ I learned that the rhyme is there in the theme, thought, and image, themselves. I learned that there is a beyond to every place — and the bird moving through the air by successive dartings taught me.

❡ It is very hard to go beyond your public. If they are satisfied with your poor performance, you will not easily make better. But if they know what is good and delight in it, you will aspire, and burn, and toil, till you achieve it.

❡ No man can write anything who does not think that what he writes is for the time the history of the world; or do anything well who does not esteem his work to be of importance. My work may be of none, but I must not think it of none, or I shall not do it with impunity.

❡ Traveling is a fool's paradise. Our first journeys discover to us the indifference of places. At home I dream that at Naples, at Rome, I can be intoxicated with beauty and lose my sadness. I pack my trunk, embrace my friends, embark on the sea and at last wake up in Naples, and there beside me is the stern fact, the sad self, unrelenting, identical, that I fled from. I seek the Vatican and the palaces. I affect to be intoxicated with sights and suggestions, but I am not intoxicated. My giant goes with me wherever I go.

ℂ The fate of my books is like the impression of my face. My acquaintances, as long back as I can remember, have always said, "Seems to me you look a little thinner than when I saw you last."

ℂ What would it avail me, if I could destroy my enemies? There would be as many tomorrow. That which I hate and fear is really in myself, and no knife is long enough to reach to its heart.

ℂ I could not possibly give you one of the "arguments" you cruelly hint at, on which any doctrine of mine stands. For I do not know what arguments mean in reference to any expression of a thought. I delight in telling what I think, but if you ask how I dare say so, or why it is so, I am the most helpless of mortal men.

ℂ Only so much do I know, as I have lived. Instantly we know whose words are loaded with life, and whose not.

ℂ To go into solitude, a man needs to retire as much from his chamber as from society. I am not solitary whilst I read and write, though nobody is with me. But if a man would be alone, let him look at the stars.

RELIGIONS & SECTS

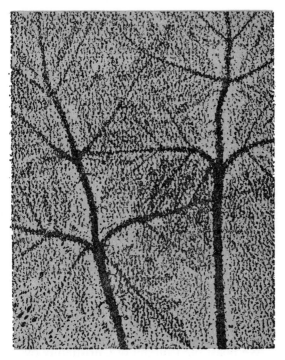

❦ The religion of one age is the literary entertainment of the next. We use in our idlest poetry and discourse the words Jove, Neptune, Mercury, as mere colors, and can hardly believe that they had to the lively Greek the anxious meaning which, in our towns, is given and received in churches when our religious names are used.

❡ We all give way to superstitions. The house in which we were born is not quite mere timber and stone; is still haunted by parents and progenitors. The creeds into which we were initiated in childhood and youth no longer hold their old place in the minds of thoughtful men, but they are not nothing to us, and we hate to have them treated with contempt. There is so much that we do not know, that we give to these suggestions the benefit of the doubt.

❡ I like the silent church before the service begins, better than any preaching. How far off, how cool, how chaste the persons look, begirt each one with a precinct or sanctuary! So let us always sit. Why should we assume the faults of our friends, or wife, or father, or child, because they sit around our hearth, or are said to have the same blood? All men have my blood and I all men's.

❡ We boast the triumph of Christianity over Paganism, meaning the victory of the spirit over the senses; but Paganism hides itself in the uniform of the Church. Paganism has only taken the oath of allegiance, taken the cross, but is Paganism still, outvotes the true men by millions of majority, carries the bag, spends the treasure, writes the tracts, elects the minister, and persecutes the true believer.

℄ Jesus Christ belonged to the true race of prophets. He saw with open eye the mystery of the soul. Drawn by its severe harmony, ravished with its beauty, he lived in it, and had his being there. Alone in all history he estimated the greatness of man. One man was true to what is in you and me. He saw that God incarnates himself in man, and evermore goes forth anew to take possession of his World. He said, in this jubilee of sublime emotion, "I am divine. Through me, God acts; through me, speaks. Would you see God, see me."

℄ Thus was he a true man. Having seen that the law in us is commanding, he would not suffer it to be commanded. Boldly, with hand, and heart, and life, he declared it was God. Thus is he, as I think, the only soul in history who has appreciated the worth of man.

℄ But what a distortion did his doctrine and memory suffer in the same, in the next, and the following ages! The understanding caught this high chant from the poet's lips, and said, in the next age, "This was Jehovah come down out of heaven. I will kill you, if you say he was a man." The idioms of his language and the figures of his rhetoric have usurped the place of his truth; and churches are not built on his principles, but on his tropes.

❦ The test of a religion or philosophy is the number of things it can explain: so true is it. But the religion of our churches explains neither art nor society nor history, but itself needs explanation.

❦ Our age is retrospective. It builds the sepulchres of the fathers. It writes biographies, histories, and criticism. The foregoing generations beheld God and nature face to face; we, through their eyes. Why should not we also enjoy an original relation to the universe? Why should not we have a poetry and philosophy of insight and not of tradition, and a religion by revelation to us, and not the history of theirs?

❦ The clergy are as like as peas. I cannot tell them apart. It was said: They have bronchitis because they read from their papers sermons with a near voice, and then, looking at the congregation, they try to speak with their far voice, and the shock is noxious. I think they do this, or the converse of this, with their thought. They look into Plato, or into the mind, and then try to make parish mincemeat of the amplitudes and eternities, and the shock is noxious. It is the old story again: once we had wooden chalices and golden priests, now we have golden chalices and wooden priests.

❡ We accept the religions and politics into which we fall, and it is only a few delicate spirits who are sufficient to see that the whole web of convention is the imbecility of those whom it entangles — that the mind suffers no religion and no empire but its own.

❡ In all my lectures, I have taught one doctrine, namely, the infinitude of the private man. This the people accept readily enough, and even with loud commendation, as long as I call the lecture Art, or Politics, or Literature, or the Household; but the moment I call it Religion, they are shocked, though it be only the application of the same truth which they receive everywhere else, to a new class of facts.

❡ We must trust the perfection of the creation so far as to believe that whatever curiosity the order of things has awakened in our minds, the order of things can satisfy. Every man's condition is a solution in hieroglyphic to those inquiries he would put. He acts it as life, before he apprehends it as truth. In like manner, nature is already, in its forms and tendencies, describing its own design. Let us interrogate the great apparition that shines so peacefully around us. Let us inquire, to what end is nature?